FOREWORD:

Teddy Anderson was raised in a Baha'i family and has a multicultural background and upbringing. In the
and grandparents were adopted into the Tlingits of the Yukon Territory in Canada. After his immediate f
Africa to Canada he attended Maxwell International School on Vancouver Island. During his summers vis. ____ ____father,
he wanted to learn the Hoop Dance, especially after I had hoop danced at his grandmother's potlatch and memorial gathering.
It was there where the traditional Hoop Dance called out to Teddy. He was invited to attend the Red Deer Aboriginal Dance Troupe
and started coming out to our sacred ceremonies as well. There was never an issue of whether Teddy shouldn't learn the dance of
our culture because he was not Aboriginal. He was invited to learn the dance because he LOVED to Hoop Dance and LOVE sees
no skin colour.

Teddy's heart was pure in his intent. He came to me with his father with a proper cultural protocol of a gift, and tobacco. Their offering was
accepted and Teddy's training began. Soon thereafter, he started getting his own outfit together. After several sessions, he started to
perform the hoop dance and was initiated at the first Red Deer traditional Pow Wow. Teddy has been very fortunate to learn from America's
foremost hoop dancer Kevin Locke, who also taught Teddy many teachings and hoop moves from his version of the traditional Hoop Dance.

At the age of 15, Teddy was becoming like a member of my own family unit, and soon after, we saw him as part of my extended family.
Shortly before Teddy took his hoop dancing full-time, he moved back to Red Deer where he began working for the Red Deer Native
Friendship Society as a youth coordinator and started teaching hoop dancing in the community.

Teddy's service to youth, children, and communities is invaluable and helps Native and non-Native children alike learn our sacred dance.
He gives back to the community by sharing his style of dance and bridging the gaps between cultures. Teddy has taught thousands of children
this dance in places around the world where our dance has never been before. Teddy's intent is to spread the oneness of humanity through
his hoops and teach the message of peace and unity of all Nations. Our family is proud of Teddy's accomplishments and travels. Any school
out there that brings Teddy in as an artist in residence is truly lucky. Enjoy Teddy's book and welcome him to your community. Witnessing
Teddy's dance is truly an unique and inspirational experience. I hope each one of you gets the chance to do so.
Miigwich (Thank you in Ojibway),
Scott Eagledog Ward

TO WHOM IT MAY CONCERN,
For over 20 years I have known Ted Anderson to honor and perpetuate his family tradition of upholding the unity and nobility of the human
spirit in every way. For the past several years Ted has been invoking the original intent of the Indigenous North American hoop dance;
a choreographed prayer to restore wholeness, balance and unity physically, mentally, emotionally and spiritually on not just an individual
basis but collectively.
Warm regards,
Kevin Locke (Lakota)

2017 APPROVAL GIVEN BY ELDER:
Tokaheya Inajin - Kevin Locke
(First to Rise)

2014 APPROVAL GIVEN BY ELDER:
Matowaykanchantewashte - Dewayne Ward
(Sacred Bear Spirit Good Heart)

The Medicine Wheel
Stories of a Hoop Dancer

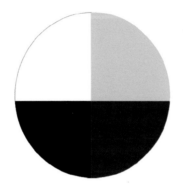

Written by: Teddy Anderson

Illustrated by: Jessika von Innerebner

A young boy, sitting with his Mooshum (Grandfather),
asks a very important question:
"Mooshum, what's that wheel around your neck?"
"That's the Medicine Wheel," says his Mooshum.

"What's the Medicine Wheel?" the boy asks.

3

"Why don't you go get the others, and I'll tell you a story," says his Mooshum.

"OK, Mooshum," says the boy.

The boy hops on his horse.
He rides all around the world picking up his friends.
Excited to hear his Mooshum's story,
he gallops as fast as he can.

The young boy and his friends soon return to the place where Mooshum is waiting for them.

"I want to tell you a story about the time before the world was one, before the end of war, and before the end of hate," explains the Mooshum.

"This is the Medicine Wheel. Many First Nations people of North America use this symbol to live a life of harmony.
Do you see how the four colours work together as one?"

9

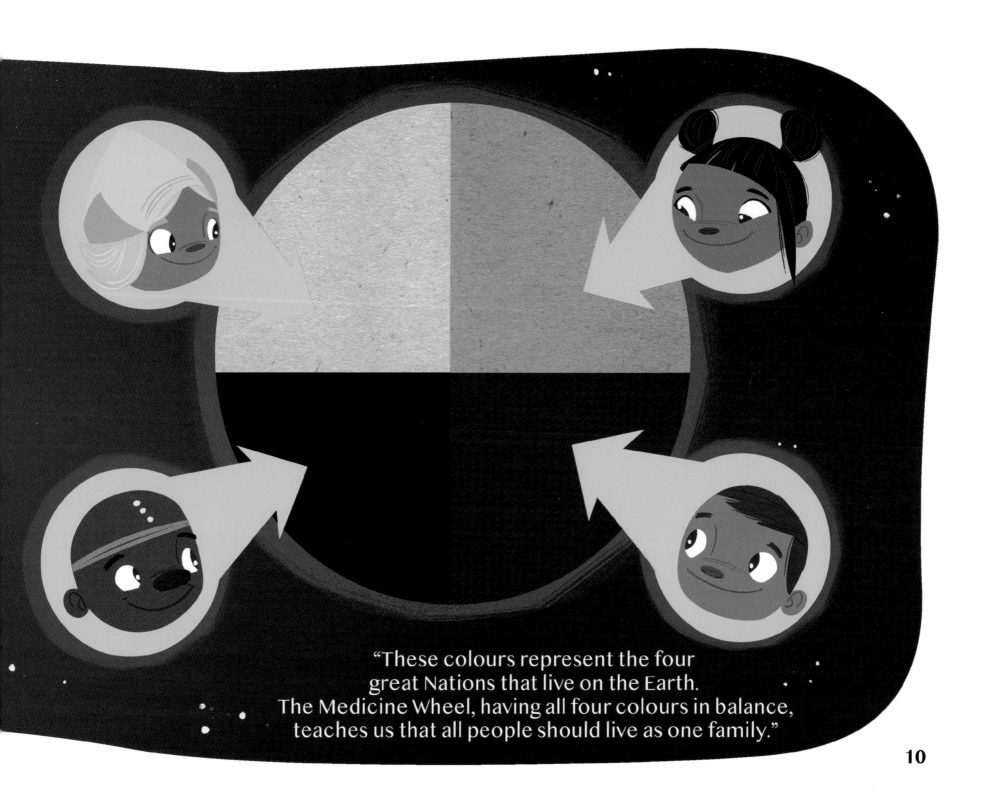

"These colours represent the four great Nations that live on the Earth. The Medicine Wheel, having all four colours in balance, teaches us that all people should live as one family."

"There once was a Hoop Dancer who saw the Medicine Wheel in this way. He used the teachings of the Medicine Wheel to unite the people and nations of the world."

11

"The Hoop Dancer taught us there is no darkness in people. Like the sun that is always shining, we must see the light and good in every single person."

13

"The Hoop Dancer taught us to help one another. He taught us to walk the path of love and friendship."

"He taught us that at the end of the path,
we will live together as one family."

16

"The Hoop Dancer taught us to be aware of our roots. He taught us to remember who we are and where we come from."

"When we do this, we grow tall and proud like trees. When we do this, we stand on Mother Earth like a mighty forest."

"The Hoop Dancer taught us to learn
from our elders, as well as our teachers and friends."

"When we use this knowledge to help other people, we blossom like beautiful flowers."

"The Hoop Dancer taught us that at the end of our journey, no matter where we come from, we all belong to one human family."

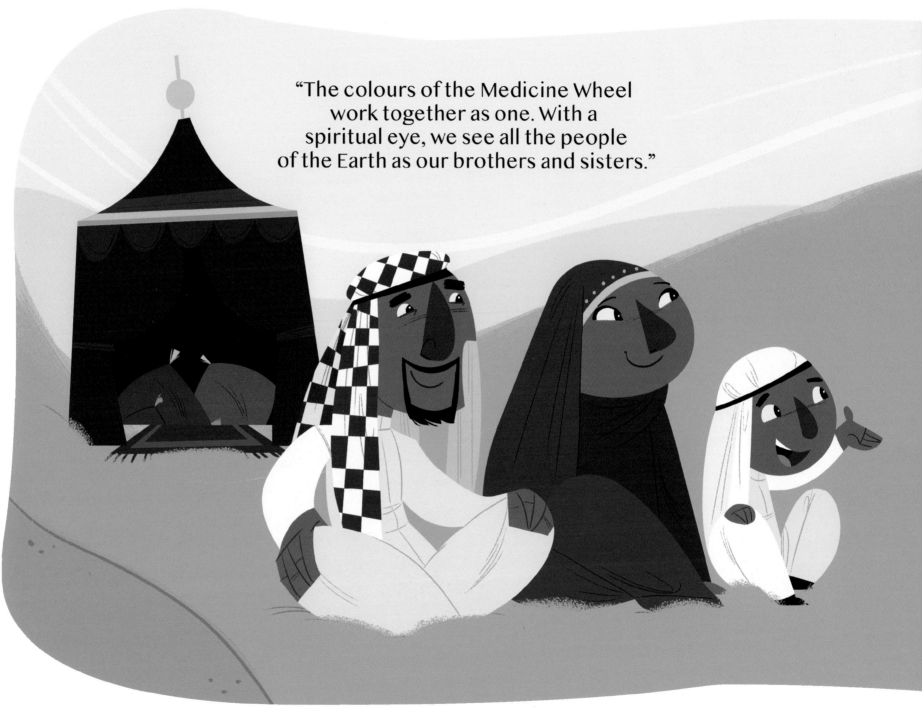

"The colours of the Medicine Wheel work together as one. With a spiritual eye, we see all the people of the Earth as our brothers and sisters."

"The people of the world are like
the colours of the Medicine Wheel."

"When we remove one,
the balance is lost."

26

"The Hoop Dancer taught us that together there is nothing we cannot accomplish."

"Together, we can build a beautiful world, where every person is equal."

28

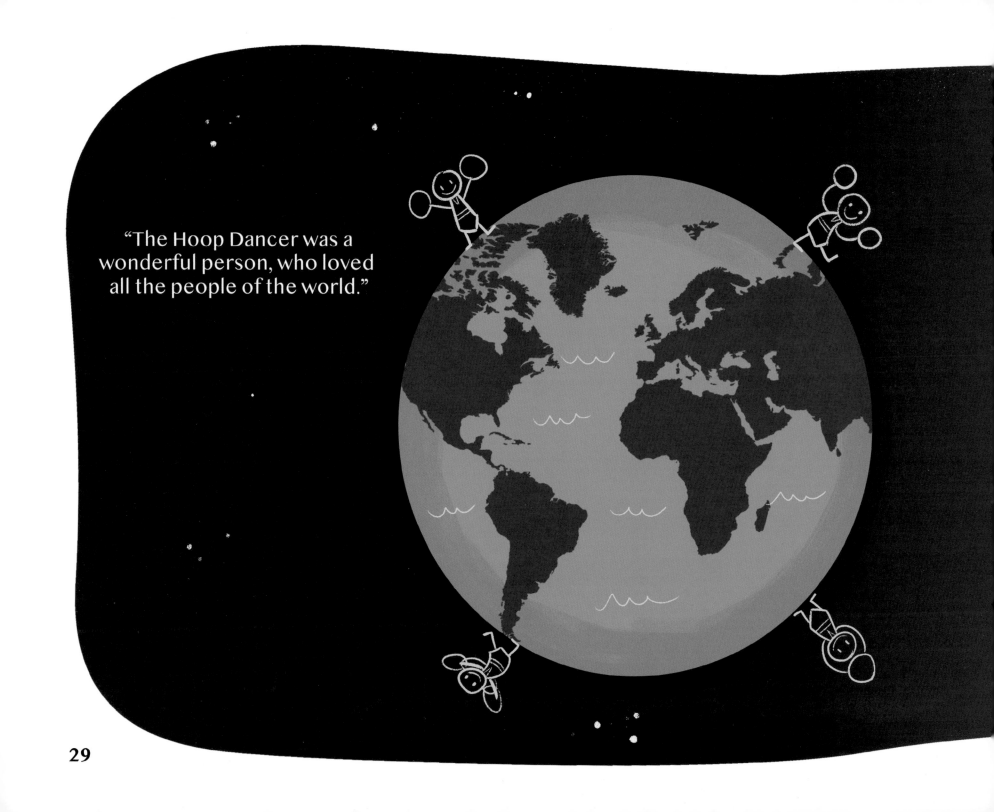

"The Hoop Dancer was a wonderful person, who loved all the people of the world."

"He had a hoop to tell his story and a heart full of hope."

30

"Mooshum, who was the Hoop Dancer?"
asks the boy.

"The Hoop Dancer was every child who grew up to change the world, to take the lessons of the Medicine Wheel into their hearts, and make the world a better place."

"It was every boy and girl, from every land, who decided they wanted a future of unity, love, and light."

34

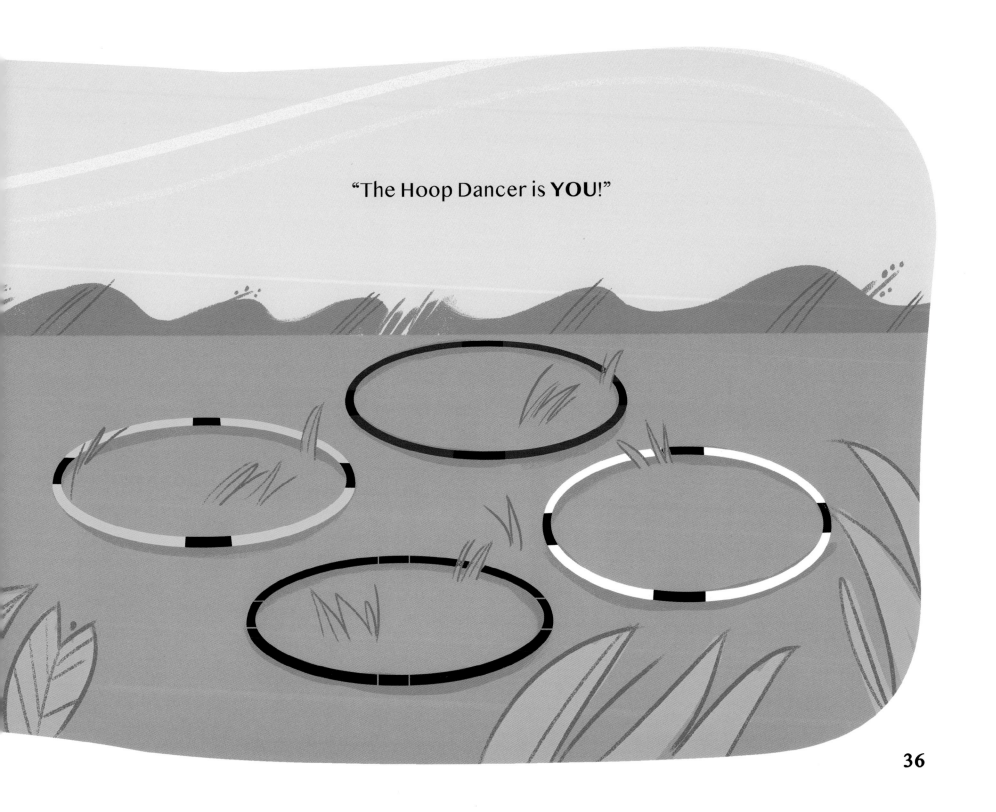

"The Hoop Dancer is **YOU!**"

36

About the Author:

Teddy Anderson is an internationally recognized hoop dancer who has performed in thousands of places around the world. He has brought his motivational message of love and unity to more than 20 countries, inspiring children and youth everywhere to see themselves as members of one human family.

When Teddy was 15-years-old, he was given special permission to hoop dance by offering ceremonial tabacco to a local hoop dancer. Since then Teddy has trained with Lakota hoop dancer Kevin Locke and recieved his blessing to continue to dance. Teddy and his family have been adopted into the Tagish/Carcross First Nation's. Teddy belongs to the Deishitaan cl and given the name Yéił S'aaghí (Crow Bones). Teddy's mother is Persian and his father is of European descent. This rich cultural experience, combined with his passion for the arts makes him unique in delivering the message of unity and inclusion.

Teddy holds a BA in Child and Youth Care and has worked for various Aboriginal agencies across Western Canada. He offers educational performances, workshops, and artist-in-residence programs on a full-time basis. When Teddy is not on tour you will find him with family, hiking, fishing, and volunteering in the community.

Curriculum

The Medicine Wheel is a lens through which students and teachers can appreciate the traditions of First Nation's people. Its stories differ depending on who tells them, but all of these tales share a common vision of unity, cooperation, and balance. The four colours represent four great tribes of the Earth. More importantly, the wheel demonstrates the need for all people and nations of the world to work together as one human family.

About the Illustrator:

Rumour has it, Jessica von Innerebner was born with a crayon in her hand. An illustrator with a passion for colour and comedy, she can draw her way out of almost anything! What she loves most is bringing engaging visuals to kid-oriented projects. Jess started her career at the age of 17, and has worked on colourful, creative ideas for Disney, Pixar, Atomic Cartoons, and Fisher Price. In spare moments, she can be found longboarding, practicing yoga, traveling to distant lands, laughing with her friends...and sometimes at them!

More Books and Resources:

Visit us at www.medicinewheel.education to learn more about our books, teacher lesson plans, etc...

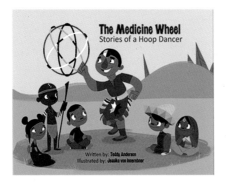
The Medicine Wheel
Stories of a Hoop Dancer
Written by: Teddy Anderson
Illustrated by: Jessika von Innerebner

RAVEN'S FEAST
Written by Kung Jaadee · Illustrated by Jessika von Innerebner

The SHARING CIRCLE
Written by Theresa "Corky" Larsen-Jonasson · Illustrated by Jessika von Innerebner

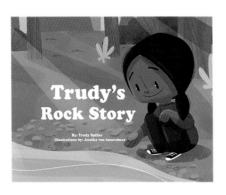
Trudy's Rock Story
By: Trudy Spiller · Illustrations by: Jessika von Innerebner

The Orange Shirt Story

Dawn FLIGHT
A Lakota Story
Written by Kevin Locke · Illustrated by Jessika von Innerebner

Books for ages 7-12 (available in English and French)

Educational lesson plans and posters available online!